T0208895

To *Jennye*

(What I Want My Little Sister to Know)

MICHELLE MOSES

WESTBOW
P R E S S®
A DIVISION OF THOMAS NELSON
& ZONDERVAN

WestBow Press books may be ordered through booksellers or by contacting:

WestBow Press
A Division of Thomas Nelson & Zondervan
1663 Liberty Drive
Bloomington, IN 47403
www.westbowpress.com
1 (866) 928-1240

ISBN: 978-1-9736-8488-6 (sc)
ISBN: 978-1-9736-8487-9 (hc)
ISBN: 978-1-9736-8489-3 (e)

Library of Congress Control Number: 2020902081

Print information available on the last page.

WestBow Press rev. date: 02/13/2020

Dear Jennye,

This book is for you. It contains all kinds of things I think any teenage girl should know. Things I wish I'd known when I was your age. And the things I'm going to share with you in this book are from a big sister's perspective. They aren't from a mother's perspective or a friend's. They are from a big sister's point of view.

The words on these pages are intended to help you, guide you, teach you, and let you know that you are not alone. There have been others before you with the same problems, and there will be others after you with the same problems. The only difference is how you choose to handle different situations. And that's why I'm here—to help you get through them in the best possible way.

So let's begin this wild ride that starts at about age ten or so and goes until well beyond your last year of being a teenager. Let the adventure begin. Hang on, little sis, here we go.

Preface

When I wrote *To Jennye*, I was single, with no kids. I had the privilege of being in the Big Brothers Big Sisters program during this time, and Jennye (pronounced *Jenny*) happened to be the little sister I was assigned. She was eleven at the time. Spending time with her and seeing her challenges, struggles, and dreams helped me write this book.

Now, years later, I have three daughters of my own (Who would have guessed—I always thought I'd have boys). Recently, I presented my oldest daughter with a copy of the manuscript to get her opinion and to subtly pass on my wise advice "from a sister's standpoint." She wouldn't read it, not even with my gentle encouragement and hints (on more than one occasion.)

I have a feeling this could happen in your household too. If you are a young girl, close to being a teen, or already one, and you are reading this book, hooray! I'm proud of you. Read on. However, as much as the intent of this book was for girls to read it, I have a feeling that some won't, and the mother or other caring friend or relative who purchased the book will be left standing there with the unopened book in their outstretched hands, hinting and suggesting to no avail.

That's okay. Go ahead, mom, dad, friend, aunt,

grandparent, whoever. Read it. Then take the things you learned and gained and pass them on to the unwilling reader. Start discussions. Foster love, concern, and an attitude of caring. I can almost guarantee that she will then come back and read it—someday. And hopefully, you'll be around when she gives her sincere, utmost, profound thanks.

School

Okay, let's start with school. It's the one thing in your life that you can't avoid. You have no choice—it's the law. And besides, how else are you going to learn?

School itself isn't really a problem. Some classes are tougher than others, some have more homework than others, and some are just more fun than others. But you can do it, and you have to start disciplining yourself to study and get your priorities straight. There are a few basic points that I want to make here.

1. Don't waste time. Get to work. Now. Get whatever it is you need to do done, and then you can play. You'll learn later in life that the days seem to get shorter and shorter and you have more and more to do.

2. Take studying seriously. Getting good grades *is* important. It's true that you can get by in life even if you get bad grades. But getting good or even *outstanding* grades will push you farther ahead in many, many ways. So make every effort to do quality work, and good grades will follow. If you need quiet solitude to study, then do what you can to get it. Lock yourself in your bedroom or the bathroom or a closet if you have

to. If studying in total silence bothers you, play some music that won't be too distracting and study to that. Do whatever works the best for you, not someone else, and *focus*.

3. Respect your teachers. Sometimes it's hard because not every teacher is great. Some may not even be all that smart. But *do* respect them. They are giving a lot of themselves by coming into your world every day. It takes a special person to be a teacher, so respect them and treat them kindly. Do what they tell you, listen to what they say, and remember that they, too, are humans. They have faults and shortcomings, just like everybody else. But they're trying, and virtually *all* of them want you to be happy and successful.

4. Participate. Part of what makes school more enjoyable is the activities that are available to you, like sports, music, plays, and clubs. Be a part of them. Try any of them. Try all of them. Try something you don't know anything about just for the experience. If you don't like it, you don't have to do it again. But at least try *something*.

A Word on Quitting

Quitting has, and always will be, one of my pet peeves. Maybe you don't even know what a pet peeve is. A pet peeve is something that bothers or annoys you very much. Quitting is one of my number one pet peeves because I believe that once you start something, you should finish it.

Teaching kids not to quit is an area that parents are responsible for in many ways. But many parents don't instill and enforce this principle, and their kids go through life beginning many new and different things and then quitting after a short time—sometimes never even giving the things a chance.

Let's take band, for example. You decide to play the drums in the band, but then you decide it's not all that great. It's work. You have to practice, and it takes some time. You decide to quit. What have you accomplished? Nothing really. You didn't stay in band long enough to learn anything, and you let both the other band members and the instructor down. What could you have done differently? You could have stuck it out the whole year. Then, after a year, if you still didn't like it, you wouldn't have to join next year. But don't quit in the middle of the year. Being seen as a quitter in anything is not a good thing.

There are only a few exceptions to the not quitting rule, in my opinion. The exceptions would be that it's okay to quit something that is dangerous or harmful to you. That is okay, and in those situations, I encourage, if not beg you, to quit. Immediately!

Okay. All that's easy enough. But what about the other parts of school that can be so frustrating? Like having to get along with everyone? First of all, getting along with *everyone* is impossible. There will be people you don't like and people who don't like you. That's just the way it is. But what you can control is how you let it affect you. You don't have to let things bother you. Sometimes things will bother you, but the sooner you get over it, the sooner your life will open up to better things. Trust me on this.

When I was in the eighth grade, I was thirteen years old. For some reason, several of the girls in my class decided that it was the year to pick on Michelle (I think it was because my boyfriend also happened to be the boy that one girl liked and she was jealous). So the girls ganged up and stuck mean notes in my locker, said mean things to me, or just wouldn't talk to me. Once, they even stole my basketball uniform on the day of a game. I told the coach that it was missing, and he told the rest of the team that it had better show up before game time, or else. And it mysteriously reappeared before the game.

Little things like that went on all year. But you know what I did? I just spent time with people who weren't mean. One girl, in particular, and I ended up developing a close friendship that continued through the years.

Don't let them bother you. Don't let them get you down. Fight back. Not with fists or angry words.

Fight back by showing them that it doesn't bother you. Because that's what they really want—they want to get to you and make you uncomfortable. Won't it be a surprise to them when you turn the tables and make them feel uncomfortable when they realize they aren't so powerful?

No matter what new challenges school brings to you, try to make the best of each and every day. Your years in school will be some of the best you ever have. It's a time when you don't have to worry about holding down a job, supporting a family, or running a household. Enjoy these times. You'll get through them just fine, and someday you'll look back at the many memories and wish you could go back again.

Getting Organized

Are you an organized person? Many people aren't. But being organized is something you can teach yourself that can help you get through life a little easier. Not only will being organized give you more spare time, but also it will eliminate a big source of stress. Here are a few things you can do that might help.

1. Make lists. Make a list of things you need to do in the order of their importance. Keep your list nearby and look at it often, crossing each thing off as it gets done. Do this every day or at least on days when you have a lot going on. This will keep you from forgetting to do something and will also let you see all that you have accomplished.

2. Plan your calendar. Get yourself a calendar that has large squares that you can write in. Keep it in a place where you can see it and use it to keep track of all your activities. If you have a really busy family, it might be a good idea to post a calendar on the refrigerator or in a central location so that everyone can keep track of what's going on.

3. Keep things in their place. This simple little practice will save you a lot of time. If everything you use has a certain place and is put back in its place time after time, you won't have to waste your valuable time looking for it. This is especially good later on when you start driving and have to keep track of the car keys.

4. Don't let things pile up. This applies to dirty clothes, papers, trash, homework assignments, and almost anything. If you don't have enough space, use stackable shelves, crates, or boxes to keep things out of your way. If you're holding on to a lot of junk, get rid of it. Get rid of clothes you never wear or things you just don't use anymore. If it's something that could be useful to someone else, donate it to a charitable organization or your church or even have a garage sale, but don't keep it around. Unless, of course, it's something that has a special place in your heart that you'll want years from now for sentimental reasons. Keeping your life free from clutter will allow positive energy to flow into your life more easily and should also help you to *feel* more organized.

Organize your life. You'll find that just by doing the simple things I talked about, you'll have more time and less stress in your life.

Developing Hobbies

By now you have probably found some things you are interested in—hobbies that you do just for fun. The American Heritage Dictionary defines a hobby as "an activity or interest pursued outside of one's regular work and engaged in primarily for pleasure." Hobbies can include just about any activity. In fact, the possibilities are endless, but whatever your hobby is, it should be something that allows *you* to relax. And the way you relax may be entirely different than the way other people relax. To some people, it's relaxing to spend four hours mountain climbing or hopping on a bicycle and riding for fifty miles. To others, sitting in a comfortable chair and reading a good book is by far their favorite, most relaxing hobby.

In addition to being relaxing, hobbies can also be exciting, dangerous, challenging, rewarding, entertaining, creative, and even profitable. They can be done inside, outdoors, at home, or away from home. Some don't cost much; others are expensive. But like I said before, with hobbies, the possibilities are endless. There are thousands and thousands of things that you can do as a hobby. Here are a few of the many examples: reading, writing, sports of all kinds, cooking, crafts, sewing, art, collecting things, gardening, animals, traveling, and music. (Note: although video games, texting, social media, and watching stuff on your phone could be considered "hobbies," try to find something that doesn't involve electronics.)

Who knows? Maybe later on, your hobby could even become your career. That's what happened to me. All of my life, I wrote out of necessity at school and at various jobs. I also wrote on my own for fun. Eventually, I decided that I liked writing so much that I would make it my career, and—believe me—it's a great feeling to be working at a job you enjoy day after day. And that's the way it is many times. People who end up turning their hobbies into careers can be some of the happiest people around.

Hobbies are a good thing, as long as they don't interfere with your day-to-day responsibilities. Remember what we talked about earlier? About not wasting time and getting the important things done first? That also applies when it comes to your hobbies. Even though you may have a great hobby that you enjoy very much, get the boring, dull stuff out of the way, and *then* you can give more time to your hobby. Your hobby should be something that you look forward to, and it can be a good incentive to get the other stuff in your life done.

The hobbies you have now may change off and on through the years. When you're sixty years old, it's very likely that you won't be able to do the same things you did when you were fifteen or twenty. That's to be expected. But the key thing to remember is that it's always a good idea to have something that you do on the side to please yourself. So start looking now. It's another one of those things that you'll look back and be glad you did.

Planning for the Future

Choosing a career isn't easy. In today's world, there are thousands of choices for women in the workforce. As women, we're unlimited in what we can do. It's never too early to start planning for your future and what *you* want to do. Think about your hobbies. Is there any way you could turn your hobby into a career? Sure, there is. Like I said before, women are unlimited, and more specifically—*you* are unlimited. You can do anything you set your mind to. I can't stress this enough. *You can do anything you want to.* Never let fear, lack of money, your age or size, or *anything* prevent you from doing what you really want to do. You can accomplish whatever you want, and miracles can happen, if you believe in yourself, follow your heart, and ask for guidance from above. What you declare, you will achieve.

So how do you begin? Start by narrowing your interests down to two or three things, and then focus in on one that you think is the best for you. If it's in the medical field, for example, try to expose yourself to people who work in that area. Visit a hospital, read books, and interview a doctor or nurse for a school project. Talk to people. Tell a teacher at school that you want help finding information. Most teachers, if not all of them, would be more than happy to help you. If you want to be an attorney, talk to an attorney. See what they do and what's involved with their job. The best way to learn about any profession is to talk to people in that area and listen to what they have to say about it.

And, of course, there's the internet. You can find as much information as you want through that avenue. Use it. Look things up and find out all you can.

Don't worry if you change your mind along the way a few times. That's perfectly okay. Supposedly, most people change careers eight times in their lives—and you haven't even started. But it *is* a good idea to focus on a particular area of interest. That way you can be more prepared for the training you'll need when you get out of high school.

Let's talk a little bit about college. College today is very, very important. Although there are examples of people in every field that have not gone to college and have done quite well, you'll find that a majority of successful, happy people have college degrees. Attending college should become a priority for you, and something that you plan on as a definite part of your future.

Just like it's never too early to start thinking about a career, it's also never too early to start saving money for college. It's no secret that it costs a lot of money to go, but since it's now a priority for you, you'll find a way. Go to your bank and see about opening a savings account if you don't have one already. Put in a certain amount of money each month, even if it's a small amount.

Use a percentage of your allowance, birthday money, babysitting money, and so on. Also, talk to someone at your bank about other ways to invest your money, such as CDs (certificates of deposit), money market funds, or mutual funds. In those types of accounts, you basically allow the bank or investment company, to borrow your money and use it. In return, they pay you interest (bonus money) that you get to keep. You may also want to check into a 529 plan, which is a college savings plan that offers tax and financial aid benefits. Your banker can help you set up the best way to save money for college that will earn you the most interest and he or she can show you examples of how much your money can grow over the years.

If you haven't already discussed it, talk to your parents *now* about college. Find out if they are going to help pay for your college education and encourage them to start a savings account (if they haven't already) for that purpose.

A few more words about investing money. Saving and investing is a *great* idea, and the sooner you can do it, the better off you'll be. Once you see how much your money can grow, you'll be amazed at how much you can have if you start the simple approach of *saving it*. Start small if you have to, but try to get in the habit (this is a word you'll see a lot of in this book) of putting a little aside each month in an interest-bearing account. This is important. Don't just stick it in a jar on your dresser. Put it in an account so it *can work for you*. It's the easiest job you'll ever have, and once you get the hang of it, you'll love it.

Saving money, furthering your education, and starting to plan now, are all important steps to take for your future. Keep an open mind about all that's available to you, and always keep your eyes open for new opportunities.

A Word on Goal Setting

As we've already discussed, when it comes to your future, the sky's the limit! You can do just about anything with a little planning, hard work, and determination. Setting goals should be one of the first steps on your way to making your dreams a reality. Goal setting can be one of the best things to do to ensure success. *A goal is nothing more than a dream with a deadline.* Follow these three simple steps, and you'll be on your way.

1. Make a list. Write down your dreams—any and all of them, no matter how outrageous they seem.
2. Put priorities in order. Decide which of your dreams are the most important and plan how you'll go about making them happen. Also, set a date for when you want to have them completed.
3. Do the list. Put your plans into action. Work and follow through. Before you know it, you'll be scratching your goals off your list as you accomplish them, one by one. Don't waste another minute. Start setting goals for yourself.

$\mathcal{M}$anners

While you were growing up, you probably heard a lot about manners. Keep your elbows off the table. Don't talk with your mouth full. Don't play with your gum. I know, by now, you probably do know the most basic manners. There are a few things, however, that I want to make sure you learn before going out into the world on your own.

1. Say thank you. Giving thanks is a very important and powerful thing. Thanking someone verbally is a very good thing to do. How many times do you thank your mom for picking you up from school? How about thanking your teacher for spending those extra few minutes helping you with a difficult math problem? Thanking someone lets them know that they are appreciated. It makes them feel good, and it should make you feel good too.

   If you want to take it up a notch, one of the best things you can do is to write a personal thank-you note. Just the few minutes it takes is worth it. A written thank-you will be appreciated even more than a verbal one by the person you send it to. Trust me: sending written thank-yous is a very good thing to learn early in life.

2. Be appreciative. Showing appreciation is always important, especially important when someone has given you a gift or done something special for you. Show your appreciation. Even if the gift is the ugliest, dumbest thing you have ever seen, at least act happy about it. Remember: it's the thought that counts. Most of the time, a gift or gesture is from the heart and is done because you're liked. Be thankful and let the person know you're grateful. Then, when you have a chance, do something in return, not because you feel like you have to but because giving and doing for others is a great feeling. Try it—you'll see.

3. Listen and don't interrupt. When someone is speaking, give them your undivided attention. Listen, and talk only when the other person is finished with what they have to say. By doing this, you show you're interested in them (even if you really aren't), and people love to think they're interesting. Hopefully, when they're done speaking, they'll give you the same respect and listen to you in return. If they don't, they probably aren't as knowledgeable as you are in how to interact with others.

4. Be prompt. It's just good manners to be on time. Being on time is also a good habit to get into at a very young age. By being on time, you're

showing others that you care, that your own time is valuable, and that you think their time is valuable, too. This not only applies for school, appointments, and other activities, but also to things you do with your friends and family. No one (not even those who love you) likes to wait on you or anyone else. Be on time for things.

5. Do what you say you're going to do. This one is very simple, and it amounts to one thing: don't make promises you can't keep. For example, if you tell someone you'll call them back, do it. Call them back. If you tell someone you'll drop something in the mail to them, drop whatever it is in the mail. Do what you say you're going to, and you'll be considered a trustworthy, reliable person.

6. Realize that basic manners are important. Yes, it's true. Those manners that your mom hammered into your head *are* important. Paying attention to them should be something you think about, and practicing them should be something you do on a daily basis. But what if you've never been taught? What if you don't even know what proper manners are? If you don't, go to the library and check out a book on etiquette (*et'-i-cut*). It will tell you everything you need to know and more.

Habits

Okay, let's discuss habits. You know what they are—they can be any number of things. They can be good or bad, wise or unwise. The fact is, some habits should be a part of your life; some should not.

Let's start by talking about the so-called "bad" habits. Bad habits include little annoying things that you may not even be aware that you are doing. Here are a few examples: biting or picking at your fingernails, jiggling your legs, saying certain words over and over (like "you know" or "um"), picking your nose, making mouth noises, flipping or twisting your hair, cracking your knuckles, and so on. You get the point.

And the point I want to make here is this: Pay attention to what you do and say. If you're doing something that could be considered annoying or offensive to someone, think twice about it. Do you want to be remembered as the girl who picked her nose? No, you don't. So pay close attention to those things, and do what it takes to stop doing them.

Sometimes that's easier said than done, but what you need to do is stop and think about what you're doing and why you're doing it. Is it because you are nervous? Is it because you're bored? Are you looking for attention? Whatever the reason, only you can determine why you're doing it, and only you can make a conscious decision to change that behavior.

If you pick at or bite your fingernails, try keeping them neatly trimmed and manicured, so you'll want to show them off. You'll be so proud of them that you'll want to show them off in a positive way, not by nibbling on them or picking at your cuticles.

If you crack your knuckles, make it a point to notice yourself doing it. And stop yourself. If you have to, ask someone you know to tell you every time you do it. Paying attention to what you are doing will pay off, and you'll be able to stop.

Some other bad habits that you may not even realize are habits include things like drinking too much soda pop, eating too much junk food, and of course, the dangerous things such as smoking, drinking alcohol, and using drugs. We'll get into those last three in another chapter. Even laziness and procrastination are nothing but habits.

The most important thing to remember is to be aware of what you're doing when you're doing it so you can control it and stop it if it's becoming a bad reflection on who you are. You and only you can take control of your life and your future by changing the negative habits that you have and turning them into more positive ones.

Let's talk now about good habits. Not only are there bad habits that are a bad reflection on you and your image, but also there are also good habits that have the opposite effect. What are some of them? There are lots of them, and here are a few examples: eating right, exercising, drinking plenty of water, taking good care of your skin, getting enough rest, doing kind things routinely, helping around the house, doing homework before playing, and so on. You get the point? Sound boring? Okay, maybe a little. But trust me and my years of experience: these things are important, good habits to get into. Why? Because later on you'll be so glad you did. Start now doing these things, and you'll be much happier later on. You'll thank yourself (and maybe even me) someday.

They say that it takes six weeks for something to become a habit and that if you do something consistently for that length of time, it will become a habit. That's not too hard to do. Try it. Pick one thing you want to work on and try doing it (or not doing it) for six weeks. Use a calendar that you keep in plain sight and mark off the days until six weeks have gone by. Don't skip a day unless you have to. Watch your progress. And then celebrate. When you're ready, try a new one. It's easy, it's fun, and you'll find that you can be very proud of yourself for what you can accomplish.

Note: As with anything, don't get down on yourself if you mess up now and then. If you're trying to quit drinking soft drinks, for example, and you give in to temptation one day and drink a big glass, don't worry.

Don't get mad at yourself. Yeah, you messed up, but it's okay. You can pick up right where you left off before. Just don't let it get to you. Remember: you are more powerful than any habit.

Protecting Yourself

Unfortunately, in today's world, crime is an issue that everyone must think about at one time or another. And at one time or another, nearly every person will become a victim of some type of crime. So what can you do to protect yourself? For starters, be alert. That's one of the most important things you can do. When you are walking alone, look around you. Try to keep yourself out of situations where you are walking alone, especially after dark. Walk with a group of people, if possible. Don't leave your purse lying around unattended or in plain view in a vehicle. Don't flash cash or talk about how much money you're carrying. At all times, watch what's going on around you. If something looks suspicious, it probably is. Trust your inner instincts, and when you feel the hair stand up on the back of your neck, pay attention.

When you're home alone, keep the doors locked and never, ever let strangers into your house when you're alone, no matter what they tell you. Criminals don't always look bad. Most of them look like average people, and they act very nice. That's how they lure people into their traps.

What if someone forces you to get into a car with them? Getting into a car with someone you don't know is one of the most dangerous things you can do, and you should avoid it at all costs. Statistics show that the chance of getting killed significantly increases when you get into a vehicle with a criminal. Even if the person has a gun, don't get in. Run, don't walk, away from there as fast as you can, and notify authorities.

I used to work in law enforcement and we were taught this hypothetical scenario: If you run away, there's only a 50 percent chance that the person will shoot at you. If he shoots at you, there is only a 50 percent chance he will hit you. If he hits you, there's only a 50 percent chance that it will be life-threatening. And if it *is* life-threatening, there's only a 50 percent chance that you'll die. So think about it. Isn't it much better to challenge those odds than to get in? Yes, it is.

It's always a good idea to be cautious. I'm not saying that you need to go through life always looking over your shoulder in constant fear, but I am saying to be alert, observant, and careful. You can and should do everything you can to protect yourself—and others.

A lot is said these days about being careful online. Don't give out personal information to someone you don't know, especially your address, financial information, passwords, or any other information that could be used to hack you. Don't "friend" people you don't know, and don't ever post things you'll regret later. Really. Don't. Do. It. Because it *can* come back to haunt you, and probably will.

Smoking, Drinking, and Drugs

Even at your young age, you've probably been exposed to several forms of tobacco, e-cigarettes (vapes), alcohol, or drugs. Some of your friends may have tried one or more of them. You may have tried one or more of them, but I strongly hope that you haven't become too attached. Here's why. Each substance mentioned above is highly addictive. In fact, it's said that cigarettes can be more addictive than many drugs. According to www.abovetheinfluence.com, your body and your mind can become addicted and crave the substance even after using it *only occasionally.*

I'm sure you have already heard the health hazards involved with each one. These aren't just scare tactics created by some overly concerned mother. These are actual facts based on studies and research. And from the research, it's plain to see that each and every one of them is harmful and can even kill you. The simple truth is that they just aren't good for you.

Another good reason not to get involved with tobacco, vaping, drugs, and alcohol is that using them can mean breaking the law. Although tobacco, in any form, and alcohol are not illegal drugs, you can get into some major trouble for using them when you are underage. Many states are cracking down on stores that sell cigarettes, tobacco products, or vapes to minors, and the stores that get caught are getting into big trouble. Lots of schools prohibit smoking on school grounds or within a certain distance of school property. Drinking alcohol is illegal for anyone under the legal drinking age. And you can get in the biggest trouble of all for using illegal drugs like marijuana, meth, crack, or heroin. Though several states have now legalized marijuana, it's still illegal to use it when you are under the legal age.

So why would anyone want to use or abuse substances? Good question. A lot of times, people start using in an attempt to try to impress someone. They think because they're doing something new and different that's also dangerous and illegal, that they are really cool. In fact, just the opposite is true. They aren't cool. They're losers. They don't have enough confidence in themselves to be happy with who they are. They are seeking outside ways to make people like them. In many cases, their attempt will backfire, and they'll be pushed away even more by the very people they were trying to impress.

I want to tell you a story about a good friend of mine named Irel. Irel was like a grandma to me as I was growing up (she was in her sixties when I was born), and I loved to spend time with her. She was funny and smart and did things with me that my real grandmas never did, like take me swimming and sunbathing, rock hunting, and horseback riding. As I got older, I enjoyed spending time with her, just visiting about old times and memories.

Irel had been a nurse when she was young, and she had many, many stories of her days working in that profession. She also told me about other parts of her life, and once, she told me something about smoking that really impressed me. In the days when Irel was young, no one really knew the health hazards associated with smoking. A lot of people smoked, including Irel, and didn't think a thing about it. But then research began to show that smoking was unhealthy. It could cause cancer and other problems. So Irel quit. Just like that. She learned it was bad for her, and she quit. Isn't that wise? Today, we know the dangers of smoking, but people choose to ignore the facts. Please, please don't ignore them any longer.

Another reason that some people start using and abusing substances is that they're extremely unhappy with their lives. They use alcohol, drugs, or even cigarettes and vapes as an escape. They let the drugs cloud their minds so they don't have to face their problems. What they don't realize is that they're making their problems even worse. The problems won't just disappear because they got drunk or smoked weed. The problems will still be there when they come down from their high, only many times they become even worse because the drugs start to interfere in other ways: missed school, failed homework assignments, getting in trouble with teachers, parents, or the law or physical problems associated with the drugs.

Saying no to drugs is not that hard. It's another prime example of taking control of your own mind and body. Your body is a special, sacred thing. You only get one—ever. It's extremely important to take care of the one you have, and one good way to do that is to stay away from foreign substances that will most likely do nothing but harm it. Enough said.

Going Out and Dating

This topic is a fun one, but it can also be a major source of conflict between you and your parents. Remember that anything I tell you in this book is always subject to your parents' rules and guidelines. Your parents always have the final say, no matter how wrong you think some of their ideas might be.

Off and on through the years, you've probably had some boyfriends or certain boys that you liked more than other ones. You may have even "gone out" or "dated." Whatever you call it, you have been around boys, and you know quite a bit about them by now. You have probably even gotten certain ideas in your head about qualities and traits that you think your "perfect match" should have. That's good, and as time goes on, those ideas will become even more solid and more important as you go through life.

A lot of parents set a certain age when they will allow their children to start dating, especially if their children happen to be daughters. For some reason, it seems like boys don't get as many rules imposed on them when it comes to dating. I guess parents aren't quite as worried about protecting their sons, but they really, really want to protect their daughters. Believe me—I know. I too was, and always will be, a daughter.

Whatever your situation, keep in mind that in everything you do, your parents are just trying to protect you. They don't want to see you get hurt, and often, they don't want you to make the same mistakes they made when they were your age. So if they tell you that you can't date until you're fourteen or sixteen or in high school or whatever, you better listen and try to make the best of it. You won't believe it now, but you have lots and lots of time for dating and hanging out with members of the opposite sex.

So what about that first date? How do you act? What do you say? The first date should be a special, memorable time—a time for getting to know the person you're going out with and a time for them to get to know you. The most important thing I can tell you is to be yourself. Don't act like someone you are not. Don't say you like things just because he does. Don't be fake. If the two of you hit it off well, it will be because you like each other just the way you are. And if he doesn't like the real you, get rid of him. You wouldn't want him anyway, no matter how cute he is, how smart he is, or how good an athlete.

What if he pressures you into doing something you don't want to do? This could involve kissing, making out, physical contact, sex, or something that may be illegal or immoral. There's no reason you should ever be pressured into something you don't want to do—*by anybody*. And especially when you're on a date with someone who's supposed to care for you. Your first approach should be to say no. You know—you've heard the words "Just say no!" This is exactly the type of situation where those words apply. Tell him no to whatever it is he wants you to do that you feel uncomfortable about.

If he doesn't listen, or tries to persuade you, tell him no again. At this point, he may get mad, make fun of you, or call you a chicken or something. That's okay. Don't let it bother you. If he still persists, stand your ground. And if he uses physical force on you in any way, it's time to leave. Walk (or run) away from him and get help. If you have a phone or can get to one, call someone you trust, like a parent, older brother or sister, friend, or teacher, and have them come get you. You're in control of your body and actions at all times. Never forget that.

Anything like that just shouldn't happen on a first date. That's not how it's supposed to be. If you're made to feel uncomfortable in any way, stop and think. Is this worth it? Is *he* worth it? The answer is no. But *you* are worth it. You *are* worth being treated the way you want to be treated. Accept nothing less. You are worth the best.

Attraction to Members of the Same Sex

What if you are attracted to girls, not boys? Many of you reading this right now are thinking, *That's crazy. I'm not gay.* But there may be some others reading this who are saying to themselves, *Yes, that's the way I feel. Am I okay for having those feelings?* Yes, you're okay. You're different, but you've probably felt different for quite some time. You're very likely in the minority. Your friends huddle together and whisper and giggle about boys, but you have no interest in what they're saying. Instead, you're more interested in *them*. It's okay.

What you're feeling is who you are. Nothing anyone can say or do can change what you feel in your heart, although if you're open about your feelings, people may try. Being honest with yourself is the most important thing, and once you've done that, you can be honest with someone you trust who you know loves you. If things get difficult, don't be ashamed to get help. There are all kinds of resources out there for help—counseling, support groups, friends, your church. If you need an understanding ear, don't be afraid to seek it.

S_{ex}

There, I said it. *Sex*. A word that's most likely familiar to you but that may be difficult to define. First, it can mean your gender, whether you're a male or a female. It can also mean sexual activity or intercourse. You see it in television shows and movies, in commercials, in books and magazines, and you hear about it at school. You may or may not hear about it at home and church. You know that it can cause pregnancy and can spread AIDS and other sexually transmitted diseases. And so you wonder, *Is it good or bad? Should I ever have sex? If so, when?*

Sex is, first and foremost, a means of reproduction. It's through the act of sexual intercourse that most creatures, including humans, create new life. But humans have one distinct difference: they are the only creatures that have the capacity to enjoy sex as a pleasurable act and not just a basic animal instinct. Sex is the most intimate, greatest expression of love a married couple can share.

Unfortunately, sex has become tarnished in our society. It's tossed around carelessly and recklessly and not given respect as the precious gift that it is—a gift that's to be treasured and used with caution, reverence, and gratitude. Unwed mothers raise children by themselves, diseases get out of control, and sexual-abuse crimes continue. Sex in the world today is something that can be downright scary.

You may have friends or know people your age who have already had sex. How do you feel about it? Do you think they're in on some special secret that you'll miss out on if you don't hurry? Not really. There's no secret that you won't be able to find out about *in due time*. There's absolutely no hurry. There are many things that are worth the wait, and sex is one of them. Why run the risk of disease or pregnancy at your young age? These are things you should think about before you ever get in a position where you have to decide whether to have sex. Decide in advance what you'll say, and how you'll handle yourself.

But what if your emotions get carried away? What if you find yourself in a situation where you've crossed the line and don't feel like you can stop? First, let me remind you again: you're in control of all you do. You may have crossed the line part of the way, but there's no reason that you can't go back. The only time you can't go back is once it's already done. Then you may find yourself regretting it or facing worse consequences. So think about it first. *Carefully.*

After you have thought about it—carefully—if you're still moving forward with sex, by all means practice safe sex *and* birth control. This would include using a condom *in all cases* and using an additional form of birth control. Years ago, when I was growing up, people didn't worry about sexually transmitted diseases all that much, and they were much more careless about sex, having unprotected sex with numerous partners. Pregnancy was the biggest fear, but birth control pills came to the rescue and helped ease that one. Today, no one can afford to be careless when it comes to sex. Any and all of those things can happen—to you—even the very first time. So please be careful. Talk to someone if you need to. But be careful—and think.

Many people today are doing the smart thing and waiting to have sex until they're married or at least part of a serious, committed relationship. They haven't lost respect in the eyes of their friends and peers. In fact, they gain respect from others in many cases because they have the courage to stand up for what they believe in and not give in to temptations or peer pressure. At the right time, sex can be a truly wonderful experience that won't cause any regret or emotional trauma. It's most definitely worth the wait.

I Didn't Wait—Now What?

I'm going to tell you a story that still amazes me to this day. When I was growing up, my parents didn't talk about sex— not to me, not around the household—it was an undiscussed subject. When I got into my teens, I started dating one specific guy, and we were pretty serious. My mom took me aside one day and said these words I'll never forget. "If you're going to be having sex, you get on birth control." *Whaaaa? Whoa, Mom.*

First of all, I was offended that she would even *think* that I was having sex (which I was, although it wasn't really full-blown intercourse but about everything else that involved those body parts). I acted put out and let her know that I couldn't believe that she thought her innocent "angel" would do such a thing. She may have believed me; she may not have. But she held firm and again repeated, "Well, if you do, get on birth control."

Looking back, I realize that she wasn't a fool. She may not have known exactly what was going on, but she was prepared if it was. I just would have liked to hear her say, "You can talk to me about it, and I can help you if you get to a point where you do want birth control." I mean, did she really think that I would get myself a doctor's appointment and take care of getting on the pill—all by myself? Not happening.

My point is that some people don't wait. They start having sex and feel like they're completely ready. If this is you, don't be afraid to talk to your mom, dad, or another adult you trust. They've probably been there, done that, and can guide you to a path that's good for everyone. Be wise, be careful, and remember: sex is special and you're worth having a special first experience now and many more special experiences in the future.

Personal Grooming

Okay, the word *grooming* sounds like something you do to your pet poodle or horse. But the definition applies to members of the human race as well as the animal kingdom. The Cambridge Dictionary defines the word *groom* in this way: "to make yourself ready to be seen." So there you have it. Personal grooming would be how you go about making yourself neat, attractive, or ready to be seen.

At your age, you've probably already begun to think more about your appearance including your hair, makeup, body, and the clothes you wear. That's perfectly normal and completely okay, as long as you don't get obsessed with any of it. Spending hours getting ready for school shouldn't be necessary. Skipping meals in order to lose a few pounds shouldn't be necessary. Spending hundreds of dollars on makeup and hair care products—not necessary. So where do you draw the line? What's necessary and what's not?

You want to look nice. That's a given. But there's no reason to go overboard. As busy as you are at your tender young age, you need a routine that's quick and simple and allows you time to do more important things.

There are certain parts of grooming that should be obvious. Those include regular bathing and washing your hair, using deodorant/antiperspirant, and taking good care of your teeth by brushing and flossing (and getting regular dental checkups).

Another important part of your daily routine should include basic skin care. This is a very important thing to start thinking about *now*. Why? Because it's another one of those things where you'll thank yourself later when, at age forty (way, way down the road), you look younger than half of all the other women your age. Start by making skin care a daily ritual that you *never* miss. This would include cleansing, toning, and moisturizing your face each morning and each night before bed. Having a clean face in the morning before you put on makeup will prevent you from trapping dirt and oils underneath your makeup and will allow the makeup to act as a barrier to keep other dirt away from your skin.

Cleansing before bed is, in my opinion, the most important of all. You should never sleep in your makeup. Think of all the dirt and oil stuck to your face that's bound to get pressed into your skin as you sleep. I wash my face every night; it's something I refuse to miss. Even on those occasions when I get home very, very late, I don't go to bed without washing my face first. I've done it since I was your age, and I still do it. Honest. Do it. Starting tonight. I insist.

There are many ways to find out what your skin type is and what skin care program would work best for you. Reading and gathering information on your own is a good place to start, and then you can seek guidance from a beauty/skin-care consultant if you desire. Whatever you do, start thinking about it—*now*.

Another word about your skin. I'm not sure if it's been drilled into your head enough, so I'll say it again. Protect your skin when you're in the sun. Wear a sunscreen, especially on your face, and reapply it every few hours or after swimming or exercising. You may know older women who have dry, leathery skin and look much older than they really are. Chances are they baked themselves to a crisp when they were your age. Now look at them. Also, try to avoid getting sunburned because that can significantly increase your chances of getting skin cancer. The bottom line: take care of yourself.

Next, get a haircut that you can manage, perhaps one that can be styled as you blow-dry it. Your hair stylist can help you choose a style that will be flattering on you and can help you with techniques for styling it. If you don't like your current hair stylist, check out a new one for some fresh ideas. Another good idea is to find a picture of a hairstyle you like. Most any hair stylist should be able to duplicate it, providing your hair isn't too thick, thin, straight, curly, and so on.

Now let's talk about makeup. Many girls start wearing makeup around the time they become teenagers or sometimes a year or two before that. I don't think there's anything wrong with wearing makeup if it's done tastefully and so that it looks natural. Of course, this is between you and your parents. But if you've been given permission, and if you have the desire to, wearing makeup can be a fun thing to experiment with.

Makeup should enhance, not hide or cover up. Remember that. Use makeup to *enhance* your eyes or lips or cheekbones or nice skin. Choose colors that complement the clothing you're wearing that day. Generally, colors with blue or purple hues are considered cool colors, colors with red or orange tones are considered warm, and black, white, or gray are considered neutral. If you are unsure, ask someone, but many times you'll be able to tell if the colors blend well together just by looking.

Daytime makeup should be natural looking and not heavy. Go easy on the makeup for school and other day-to-day activities. You can use darker, more vibrant colors for evenings and special times. Find someone (possibly an older friend or relative) who you think does a good job with her makeup, and talk to her. Compare notes. Maybe even get together and do each other's makeup. (But you should never trade or use someone else's makeup or makeup brushes. This can spread disease and infection.)

Each and every person on this earth is unique. You're one of them, and you can learn to make the most of your features and enhance what you have. So spend a little time working on it. You can become an even better you.

Your Monthly Cycle

Having your period is a part of being female—a part that has historically been considered a bad thing in many cultures. Over the years, a woman's period has been called everything from "the curse" to "being on the rag." Almost all women have one or more symptoms as part of their monthly cycle, including weight gain, bloating, cramps, tender breasts, headaches, and mood swings. The level of intensity varies from woman to woman, and many women find relief simply by taking over-the-counter pain relievers.

Some women also have PMS (premenstrual syndrome). You've probably heard quite a bit about PMS, because over the years, it has become well-known and has sometimes taken a bad rap. To some, it has become a joke. To others, PMS is to blame for every emotion a woman displays. But PMS isn't imaginary. It's very real, and its symptoms are very real to those who have it. If you think you have PMS and the symptoms are disrupting your life once a month, talk to your doctor about it. It may be possible for him or her to provide you with medication to ease the symptoms.

Another thing that can help you get through each month a little easier is your attitude. Just changing your mental attitude about the issue can make a huge difference in the way you feel before, during, and after your "time of the month." Don't think of your period as a big deal. Don't let it keep you from doing things. Say to yourself that it's a good thing and believe it. Try to keep your life as stress-free as possible (stress is *never* good) during the times when you experience the biggest mood swings. The mind is an extremely powerful thing, and even the way you think about something like your period can control the way your body responds. Your monthly cycle is not fun, by any means, but each and every month can be a private reminder for you and a celebration of the fact that you're a woman capable of creating new life.

Diet and Nutrition

I'm going to guess that this is a topic you haven't thought about too much. But maybe, after reading this, you will, because in my opinion, what you eat ranks at the top (tied with mental attitude) for determining your overall health. That may be a bold statement, but think about it. Everything that you eat or drink has to be processed by your body into fuel to keep each and every part functioning. It's an amazing task.

Have you ever read a nutrition label? If you haven't, do it today. You can find labels on almost every food or drink product available, and they can be very interesting. See how many calories you're getting. Notice the fat grams. Pay attention to sodium and sugar amounts. Look at the list of ingredients. It's important to know what you are putting into your body. Start now, eating and drinking for a healthy lifestyle.

Try to eat a balanced diet. What's a balanced diet? A balanced diet consists of food from all of the major food groups, including six-to-eleven servings from the bread-cereal-rice-and-pasta group; three-to-five servings from the vegetable group; two-to-four servings from the fruit group; two-to-three servings from the milk-yogurt-and-cheese group; two-to-three servings from the meat-poultry-fish-dry beans-eggs-and-nut group;

and fats, oils and sweets used sparingly. A diet low in fat and high in fiber is also important for preventing heart disease and cancer later in life. Try to avoid too much caffeine and junk food. I believe that a good rule of thumb is to allow yourself to eat whatever you want, but to do it in moderation. That's the key. Don't starve yourself, but don't binge either. If your body is craving something, it probably really needs it. So give in, but don't overdo it.

When I was growing up, eating breakfast was considered the most important meal of the day, although now there are differing thoughts about how and when you break your fast. Maybe you're not hungry in the morning. That's okay. Have something nutritious when you feel hungry to get your mind and body going. Even if it's just a piece of fruit, a bagel, or leftovers from the night before, have something. Oh, and by the way, candy, donuts, and chips are not good suggestions for your first meal of the day.

This section wouldn't be complete without a little story about my own mother, who was almost fanatic about eating breakfast. There were many times that I just didn't want breakfast, but she made me have something anyway, even if it was just a glass of orange juice. There was no arguing. My brother and I had to have breakfast before we went to school, each and every morning. It must have worked. We both did well in school, and I don't remember ever being too sluggish or unenergetic (that comes later in life). Needless to say, eating breakfast is now a very important part of my life—something that I always do. I guess Mom was right. (Yes, as hard as it is to believe, the older you get, the more you'll realize that there are many things your mom was right about.)

What about body image? Right now, your body is changing at a rapid pace. You are growing and developing as part of adolescence. It may be hard to get used to. It may be uncomfortable, both physically and emotionally. You may even get teased about some of the changes you are going through. Just remember: you aren't the only one who's changing. Everyone else who's close to your age is going through exactly the same changes. The only difference may be in the results of those changes. Don't let the changes bother you. Accept them and love yourself for the beautiful, unique person you are. Consider the prayer of serenity: Lord, grant me the serenity (peace, patience) to accept the things I cannot change, the courage to change the things I can, and the wisdom to know the difference. Meditate on that prayer if you are having a difficult time with your body. Love yourself and know that you are a special, special part of this universe.

Exercise

Exercise is a vitally important key to staying healthy. Let me say that again: exercise is *vitally* important. It isn't just a theory; it's now a proven fact that exercise is necessary for prolonging life and preventing disease. Besides that, you'll just feel better.

So where do you begin? While you're in school, you have it made. All of the school sports are an ideal way for you to get the exercise you need as well as allowing you to be part of a group that shares the same goals and challenges. Organized school sports force you to be disciplined. You have regular practices, and you're expected to be there. That's built-in motivation. It's usually a lot easier to have someone else tell you when you're going to exercise, what you'll be doing, and for how long.

Take it seriously. This is especially important when you're part of a team sport. Not only are you trying to do your own personal best, but also you're trying to do well for the team. They all want you to give 100 percent (or as my coach used to say, 110 percent). Follow the rules. If your school has a sports curfew, obey it. And work hard at practice. Challenge and push yourself, remembering at all times that what you're doing is good for you. Sometimes it's hard, but it pays off as you get in shape, develop your reflexes and coordination, and learn to work together.

Listen to your body. With any type of exercise, it's important to listen to your body. How do you do that? Every ache and pain is a sign from your body. Your body is a magnificent creation that can handle a lot, but every body can only take so much before it starts sending signals to you to slow down. It's possible to push it too far, and what you have to do is learn to recognize when that is happening.

When you start a new exercise, or do something you're not used to, you'll often have muscle pain. That's normal. Muscle pain means that you're working and stretching your muscles. But when the pain doesn't go away after a while, you may be pushing yourself too hard. Take a little time off if you can. Give your body a chance to heal. If you experience other aches and pains that don't seem normal, try a rest first, and if that doesn't work, it may be time to see a doctor. Try to pay attention to the signs and signals from your body to your brain. Listen to them and pay attention to them if you want to prevent serious injuries later on.

What if you hate sports? What if you have zero coordination? If you absolutely don't like sports or can't participate for some reason, try to exercise on your own. There are many things you can do outside of school to stay fit. Running, walking, biking, hiking, swimming, tennis, aerobics, and weight lifting are a few good examples. Just do *something* physical. Do *not* become a couch potato at your age. If you do, chances are that habit will carry over into your adult life. Get moving, get active, and get energized.

Here's my story. Growing up, I had biked, swum, and done some gymnastics and a little bit of running, but starting in seventh grade, I went out for volleyball, basketball, and track. It was the first time I had participated in any kind of organized sport. I wasn't the best athlete, by any means, but I did okay, and I really enjoyed being a part of it all. I continued participating in sports throughout high school, going out for cross-country three years, volleyball one year, and basketball and track all four years. In between sports and during the summer, I jogged to stay in shape. Through hard work and commitment, I could see myself improve each year, and by my senior year, I felt like I was in the best physical shape I had ever been in.

After high school, my days of organized sports were over. College sports were not in the picture for me, but I knew that I wanted to continue keeping my body in the best physical shape possible. I started jogging almost every day, along with some aerobics and weight lifting. I had always hated running in the mornings. My body was usually stiff and it was harder to get going. But I found that if I made myself get up and run each morning, I got it done and out of the way, and I only had to shower once during the day. If I didn't run in the morning, it was so easy to put off and find an excuse not to do it. So guess what? I made my morning run a habit, and pretty soon, I even started to like it. Running became a way for me to get closer to nature and see first-hand what the weather was doing. Once in a while, I would challenge myself by training for and entering a race, just for extra motivation. To this day, I still exercise (now it's mostly walking and weights) five days a week, but I do let my body rest for two days, usually on the weekend. I use the time when working out to focus on and plan my day, or to think about personal issues that I need to sort out. I exercise rain or shine, in cold or hot weather. It can be tiring, and sometimes a real drag, but it can also be exhilarating and a joy to know I'm doing something so good for myself.

Looking back, I wouldn't trade my experiences in school sports for anything. Each sport taught me different things and built my self-confidence in different ways. I also shared a special kind of bond with my team members that wasn't possible with those who weren't "on the team." I'm also glad that I started early in life recognizing the importance of exercise, and I looked for ways that I could continue making it a part of my life as I got older. I encourage you to do the same thing for yourself—starting today.

Recharging Your Batteries

Just as important as it is to live an active, energetic lifestyle, it's also important to give your body the rest it needs (and deserves). Sleep is crucial to your overall health and well-being. With the right amount of sleep, you'll feel better, think better, fight off illness more easily, and get well faster if you do get sick.

As busy as you are at this time of your life, how do you make sure you get enough sleep? You have school all day, sports and other after school activities, and then homework, not to mention any activities your family has planned. First, let me remind you that life never really slows down. Through the years, you'll be just as busy, although the way your time is spent will change.

Getting enough sleep should become a priority in your life, and you can make it a priority by incorporating some of the other things we've talked about, like getting organized. Try to create a daily schedule that you can stick to. Do your homework at the same time each night (right after supper, for example). Utilize study time at school, so that you won't have so much homework in the evening. Try to go to bed at about the same time each night, and go through a similar routine each time (such as brushing your teeth and, of course, washing your face). That way, your body will recognize that you are winding down for the evening.

When you're finally able to crawl into bed, you need to make every effort to be able to get the most quality sleep that you can. Avoid things that contain caffeine (soda pop, tea, coffee, chocolate, and some medications) several hours before bed. Don't go to bed right after a heavy meal. Wear something comfortable to sleep in. Take a hot bath before bed if you need help relaxing and winding down.

Don't let your mind fill up with a lot of jumbled thoughts as you lay down to go to sleep. If there are things you need to think about, quickly run through them in your mind and then consciously put them to rest along with your body. If you are really wired for some reason, pray or meditate, or think about something that's really soothing to you.

Don't go to bed angry. Vent, cry, throw a fit, or punch your pillow. Get it out. Apologize and forgive, if necessary. Then, and only then, go to bed. You'll sleep much better getting whatever it is out of your system before you ever crawl between the sheets.

What if you can't get to sleep? There's no worse feeling than not being able to sleep. Many times, insomnia happens because there's too much on our minds and we aren't able to put the thoughts aside. Or, sometimes, there's just no explanation. We just can't sleep. That's all there is to it. A few suggestions: Try relaxing each and every part of your body. Beginning with the toes and moving upward to the top of your head, focus on relaxing each part of your body (toes, feet, ankles, calves, knees, legs, etc.), moving to the next part only when the part you're working on feels totally relaxed. This works really well and can be used anytime you're tense.

If you still can't sleep, you can try getting up for a little while. Read, write a letter or a journal entry, or listen to some music (nothing too loud or intense). Try to avoid your phone or electronic devices, as these can actually stimulate your brain. Also, don't get into the habit of getting up and eating, unless it's a *light* snack or noncaffeinated drink. Getting up for a short time should help you, and before long, you'll feel more tired and be able to go back to bed and get to sleep without much effort.

After you're asleep, you're home free, unless of course you have a bad dream or a nightmare that wakes you up in the middle of the night. Dreams can be scary, pleasant, or bizarre, but in any case, they're always fascinating. I love dreaming, and some of my dreams are very weird. But to me, dreaming is like a whole other world, where I see old friends, get into exciting adventures, and work through my problems in unique ways. Did you know that everyone dreams, every night? If you don't remember your dreams, it's because you didn't wake up while the dream was occurring. Dreams take place during REM sleep, the deepest sleep of the night, and can only be remembered if you wake up. I must wake up a lot during my dreams, because I remember them quite often. Some nights, I may remember as many as four or five different dreams.

Dreams can be used to help you and guide you through problems you may be having in your daily life. Because they're a part of your subconscious mind, dreams often hold the answer to things that you might not be able to see during waking hours. So exactly how do you tap into this inner resource? One thing you can do is focus on the issue you want to address as you go to sleep. Think about what it is you want your dreams to reveal, and tell yourself that you'll remember your dreams. Many times, this approach will work, and as you sleep, your "dream mind" will take over where your "waking mind" left off. You'll find that the more you do this, the more you'll remember, and the more you'll benefit.

Another thing that might be helpful is to keep a dream journal. This doesn't have to be anything fancy—a simple notebook will do—and it should be kept beside your bed. Jot down what you remember about your dreams as soon as you can. The longer you go without writing down the details, the more you'll forget, so try to do it right away. Then look back at your journal and see if any of the things you dreamed about symbolize things in your life. You don't always get a clear-cut answer, and sometimes, your answer will come in the way that you interpret the dream. So try looking at dreams in a different way. They can be fun *and* helpful, and can open up a whole new world for you.

The two important things to remember are: sleep and rest. Get a good amount of sleep each night, and if you have the opportunity, rest during the day when you're tired. A fifteen-minute power nap can work wonders to refresh you and get you reenergized. If you haven't been getting the rest you need, do what you can to change that. If you have to, shift your priorities around a little bit. Your mind, body, and spirit are counting on you. Sweet dreams.

Making a Fashion Statement

Maybe you've heard the expression, "You are what you wear." It's true. Your clothes do say a lot about you and the kind of person you are, so it's important to think a little bit about what you wear. This will become even more important as you become an adult and move into the workforce. Sometimes, dressing right can be the difference between getting a job and seeing it go to someone else.

Your clothing should be a reflection of your tastes, interests, and attitudes, but keep in mind that fashions change rapidly, and with the cost of clothing, it's a good idea to stay away from extremely trendy fashions. They will only be in style for a short period of time, and after that, you won't want to be caught dead in them. No matter what styles you like, the most important thing is to wear clothes that fit well. Don't squeeze into clothes that are way too tight or that are so loose they practically fall off. Think about the image of yourself that you want people to have and go from there.

Another type of fashion statement that has become quite popular for people of all ages, is body art, including body piercing and tattoos. This is another area that probably causes many heated discussions between parents and their children in households across the country. It's definitely a way to express yourself and your individuality. That's for sure.

But body art of all types is something you'll want to think long and hard about before you do it. Let's suppose your parents have said, "No, absolutely not! No tattoos while you live under my roof!" You beg. You plead. You say, "Then can I get my nose pierced?"

Again, you are met with roars of disapproval. "No! No! No! And don't bring it up again!" Okay, you get the point, and you realize that it isn't going to pay off to keep fighting it. So you've accepted the fact that you won't be able to decorate your body the way you want until you leave home.

Jump ahead. You're now twenty years old. You're off at college, on your own for the most part. A few friends decide to go to the local tattoo place and get one. You go too and end up getting a small butterfly tattooed on your ankle. No big deal. It's done, and you're happy. But did you think of the consequences before you did it? Consequences? What consequences? It's just a small little tattoo in a discreet place. What in the world is there to think about? That's what I'm here for. To get you to think about the things you might want to consider before doing the kinds of things many young people do.

Consequence one—Infection to tattooed or pierced area, or the spread of diseases such as hepatitis or HIV, caused by unsanitary needles or improper procedures. Infection can result in pain, scarring, illness, and in some cases, loss of a limb, or even death. Wow. Or perhaps your skin will have an allergic reaction to the ink/dye that is used. In any case, there are many health consequences to be aware of.

Consequence two—Tattoos and some pierced places are hard to hide if they are in highly visible locations. "But why would I want to hide it?" you say. "I got it so I could show people, not hide it." I understand, really I do. But let's just say that you get invited to some event in which you have to dress elegantly, such as a formal occasion or a wedding (maybe even your own wedding). Or let's say you are going to a job interview with an impressive, high-paying business firm. A tattoo, or something like a pierced eyebrow, is not always appropriate in some of these situations. Trust me. Just think about what I'm saying, that's all.

Consequence three—You can't take a tattoo off. Ever. There are ways, but they can be painful and costly, and not always 100 percent successful. Visualize yourself as a sixty-year-old woman. Would your tattoo still be something you want to show off then? You might even have grandkids by then. What will they think? Maybe they will think you're one hip grandma, or they might laugh at the dolphin clinging to your shoulder that's starting to get a little wrinkled and saggy. (At least with a pierced area, you can let it grow shut, but if it's been there a long time, it might not ever close completely, or it might leave scar tissue.)

Okay, enough about consequences. Just remember: any and every thing you do to your body is *your choice*, now and always.

Spiritual Issues

More and more is being discovered about the mind, body, and spirit connection. Each of us has a mind, body, and spirit. All three are separate parts that are intertwined into one whole being—you. Each part needs special care and attention. If one part is out of whack, the other parts can, and will, suffer. You can make sure you are "in tune" by taking care of your physical body, keeping your mind open and alert and filled with positive messages, and by letting your spirit guide you by listening to your intuitions.

While each of us has our own separate spirit, the word *spirit* can also be used in a religious sense. Religion is a very important part of anyone's life. I hope that you have learned that by now, but if you haven't, maybe you will after reading this book. What I'm talking about here, extends far beyond just going to church every Sunday. I'm talking about believing in a higher power. Believing in a higher power is important at any phase of your life, but especially as a teenager. Sometimes a higher power, like God, is the only place you can turn for advice, guidance, or understanding. All you have to do is ask. Turn inward and ask for help through prayer. You can do it anytime, anywhere, and about any subject. God inside of you, directing your spirit, will guide you through virtually everything.

What about going to church, worshiping as a group? If you are treating others kindly, living a good life, and praying, why do you need to go to church? There are several answers. First of all, it's good to learn about and study what others are studying.

Second, prayer is more powerful when it's shared by more than one person. And third, a church family is an extension of your own family, a support system in good times and bad. Church can be a place you go to bond with and reinforce your inner spirit, and it can also be a good place to meet other people who share your beliefs.

Is it right to pray about things like schoolwork and tests and basketball games? There is nothing that it's *wrong* to pray about. Just know that everything you pray or ask for may not be given to you. I have always liked this saying: "Some folks just don't seem to realize when they're moaning about not getting prayers answered that *no* is the answer." You may have also heard the saying, "Be careful what you pray for." That one, too, is true, and pretty much speaks for itself.

Everything that happens in your life, happens for a reason, in order to teach you a lesson. If you fail a test, maybe the lesson you are to learn is that you need to become more disciplined in your study habits, or maybe that you need to pay more attention in class. If you lose a basketball game, the lesson may be in how to lose gracefully. Maybe the other team is learning the lesson of winning. It's really a neat thing if you think about it. Nothing in your life will happen out of the blue. Everything will happen because it's supposed to for one reason or another. If you accept this principle and believe in it, your life will become much more stress-free, and you'll live with more inner peace. All you have to do is look for the lesson, and it will help you understand why things happened the way they did.

If you haven't ever gotten in touch with your spiritual side, work toward that goal. Pray more. Meditate more. Attend worship services. Read the Bible and books that can help you learn more about your inner spirit. Believe, trust, and know that with each and every life experience, you'll gain something that can be carried with you into the future.

Karma

Have you ever heard of karma? An easy way to define karma is that you receive from the world what you give to the world. The Golden Rule—do unto others as you would have them do unto you—is based on karma. In many ways, karma is a mysterious force that's hard to explain, but again and again, it proves itself to be true. A person who hates will experience hatred from others. A person who loves will experience love in life. By giving, you shall receive.

Giving. That is a very important word—a word that more or less defines what life is all about. Do you give? Maybe you're saying, "I can't give. I don't have any money the way it is." That may be true, but there are many things that you can give, besides money, that will make you feel good about yourself and make someone else feel good too. What about time? Do you have any extra time that you could give volunteering for a good cause, visiting an elderly neighbor or relative, playing with a small child that is lonely, or helping with extra chores around the house? Don't get me wrong. I know you're very busy, and I'll be the first to tell you that you need to take time for yourself once in a while. Sometimes you do need to slow down and read a book you enjoy or watch TV or listen to your new music.

But it will also make a difference in your life when you make a difference in someone else's. Try it. You'll see.

Think about karma every day. Think about what you are doing, and know that by doing good, positive things, the same will come back to you. In all you do, give, share, love, be positive, and spread joy, and you'll find that your life becomes better and better all the time.

A Word about the Power of Positive Thinking

Throughout this book, I have mentioned a lot about being *positive*. In the section on diet and nutrition, I even went so far as to say that mental attitude is at the top of the list when it comes to your health and overall well-being. I truly believe it. People who live to be one hundred often say that they credit their long lives to a positive attitude. There are countless stories of people who have actually cured their own diseases, like cancer, just by telling themselves that they can get better. Being positive can fight off illness and bring a constant flow of good things into your life.

Many people don't even realize that they are being negative because they have been programmed with negativity since they were able to talk. They pick up negative thoughts and attitudes from their parents, relatives, friends, and the media. Are you being negative without even realizing it? Here are a few examples of things you might be saying that are negative.

"I can't study." – "I'm not very attractive." – "I never get to do things." – "I'll never have any money." – "I'm terrible at sports." – "I hate going to school." – "I can't stand her." – "That makes me sick."

Those are all examples of negative statements that you may have said at one time or another. The more you say things like that, the more you'll actually believe them. And guess what? If you start saying positive things to yourself over and over again, your mind will actually begin to believe what you are telling it.

When I was your age, no one told me about this wonderful secret. I had to learn it on my own, and I wish I'd known about it much sooner. So now, I want to stress to you how important it is to think positive at all times. It will change your life, making it as good as you want it to be. There are no limitations to what you can achieve. Go for it.

Caring for the Environment

Do you ever think about the earth and what a wonderful, magnificent place it is? Whether you have or haven't, take a few minutes right now to think about this great place we live. Think about how many plants and animals live and thrive here together day in, day out. Think about the beauty of the land: the mountains and forests, the prairies, the oceans, and the sky with its ever-changing palette of colors. What a place. And it's a place that needs our constant attention and awareness.

You may think that there's nothing that you as an individual can do to make a difference in the quality of life on earth. You're wrong. There are many things you can do to ensure that the earth we live on today will be in good shape for years to come. For starters, pay attention to what you use and throw away. Never, ever litter. Never let anyone you're with litter. Every tiny piece of litter is a thoughtless sign of total disregard for our earth.

Next, recycle, recycle, recycle. Use and reuse as many things as you can, and if you are done with it, recycle it by giving it to someone who can use it or taking it to a recycling center or drop-off location.

Encourage your parents to recycle if they don't, or at least talk them into letting you do it for them.

Again, all I'm saying is be conscientious. Think about the products and natural resources that you use. Don't waste water. Shut off lights and appliances when you aren't using them. Keep doors and windows closed. Turn down your thermostats in the winter and wear an extra sweater or throw an extra blanket on the bed to stay warmer. Do what you can to conserve gas, such as carpooling to school, riding your bike, walking, and so on. Talk to people you know about doing the same things. You really can make a difference, and if everyone did just a little, it would make a huge one.

Caring for the environment also includes caring for the other animals that inhabit the earth. You and your family may have chosen to care for some animals by adopting them as additional family members. Pets can be a lot of fun and a good way to give and receive lots of love, but having a pet means being a responsible pet owner. What exactly is a responsible pet owner? A responsible pet owner takes good care of their pet by making sure it gets enough food and water, a clean, safe place to sleep or stay that's sheltered from the weather, and medical care, if necessary.

You've probably also heard that it's important to get your dogs or cats spayed or neutered. This involves a routine operation that will prevent the animal from being able to reproduce. It's important to do this. There are thousands and thousands of unwanted pets that don't have good homes. Did you know that one female cat and one male cat and their offspring results in 420,000 kittens in seven years? That's amazing—also sad. Helping to control the country's pet population is the responsible thing to do when you have a pet.

Responsible pet owners give their pets attention and love. A pet needs attention just as much as a human does. This includes petting, talking, and friendly, positive words. It also includes giving your pet the proper amount of exercise. In short, be good to your pet, and they will be good to you by being one of the most loving and loyal friends you could ever have.

Remember: you *can* play a big part in protecting the earth we live on and its many wonderful resources. Do your part and encourage others to do the same.

Driving

If you haven't reached driving age yet, you probably feel that the day will never come. You can hardly stand it. You long for the day when you can get behind the wheel and drive off into the sunset—or just to the grocery store, for that matter. If you're already sixteen or older, you're probably driving by now, and you probably love it. Everyone drives. In today's fast-paced world, someone who doesn't drive is an exception. Driving is a great thing, no doubt about it.

Even as great as driving is, there are still a few points that need to be made. First, let me say that driving is not a God-given right. It's a privilege given to people who are responsible and law abiding. It can be very enjoyable and a good, if not necessary, way to get around in today's world. So when you earn the privilege of driving by becoming legally old enough and mastering the necessary skills, you should also keep in mind the other things listed here.

1. Keep your vehicle maintained. Learn at least a little bit about car care. Listen and look for signs of trouble and get them taken care of. Get the oil changed, the fluids checked, and the tires aired up on a regular basis. Have someone show you

how to check the oil and change a tire, just in case. Keep your car clean, inside and out.

2. Drive carefully and responsibly. This includes obeying the traffic laws, wearing a seat belt at all times, and paying attention to the road (no texting, please).

3. Drive defensively. This means using your driving skills to protect yourself from bad drivers, drunk or texting drivers, and poor weather conditions. This is very important when you're out on the road. Chances are that you're the only person watching out for you. Your actions may be the difference between being safe and having a wreck—and between life and death. If another driver gets mad at you for some reason, try to remain calm and avoid responding verbally or with physical gestures. Many times by ignoring the other driver, you'll prevent a case of uncontrollable road rage that could cause a serious, or even fatal, accident.

4. Enjoy your privilege. Remember the days when you had to depend on someone else to get you where you were going and be thankful that you can now do it yourself. Have fun, but don't blow your privilege by doing something crazy or stupid.

Getting Along with Your Parents

Sometimes this one can be tough. You and your parents most likely have different views on a lot of things right now. If you don't, you're one of the lucky ones. If you're a typical teenager, you probably fight with your parents more now than you ever have about all kinds of things, like homework, your grades, boys, clothes, makeup, going out, and other things. It can be difficult for everyone involved.

So how do you go about getting along? How do you get through the teenage years without wanting to kill one another? It can be done, but it takes effort on the part of both the parent(s) and the teenager. Since this book is specifically for teens, that's what we're going to talk about. Your parents have all kinds of resources they can consult for how to get along better with you. You have this book as a guide.

First of all, don't make it more difficult than it needs to be. What do I mean by that? Getting along is a conscious choice that you can make. If you decide to get along and tell yourself that you're going to, it will be a lot easier than if you constantly play negative tapes in your head like "I can't get along with them. They're so uncool. They just don't understand. They don't care what I feel." All of those things are very negative. What you need to do is be positive. Say to yourself, or out loud if you want to, "I *can* get along. My parents are human too. They've been through a lot before I ever came along. They care and that's why they want to protect me."

Another thing you can do is *try* to understand. Try to see where they are coming from. I know that sometimes that isn't easy. But believe me when I say this: almost every parent out there wants only the best for their children. Most parents consider their children the most important things in the world, and they want to protect them, guide them, and steer them away from trouble. They don't want their children to have to experience things on their own in order to learn, although many times that's exactly what needs to happen. Many times, even the most loving, obedient kids just won't believe something until they try it or experience it for themselves. Then, more times than not, they admit that their parents were right and go on.

It goes without saying that parents aren't always right either. But as parents, your mom and dad have the responsibility of doing the best job they can to guide you successfully down the path to adulthood. They're trying. They really are. So try to get along. It will make both of your lives much smoother and much less stressed.

Communicate. Talk to your parents about what's going on in your life. Let them know what you're doing, who you're hanging out with, and what you're thinking. They want to know. They are interested in *you* and want the best for *you*. Talk to them about what emotions are going on inside your head. Maybe they have a similar situation that happened to them. Maybe they'll surprise you. Open the doors of communication. It can really, really help your relationship.

Don't forget that communication is a two-way street. In addition to voicing your thoughts and opinions, you also have to *listen*. Listening—really listening—can be difficult to do. Many people hear what's being said, but they don't really listen. Listening is often even more important than talking. That's why we have two ears and only one mouth. To communicate in the best possible way, you have to listen too.

Learn *now* how to communicate. Try to do it without yelling. Try to stay focused on the situation at hand. Don't bring up past hurts. Try to communicate in a loving, positive way. It takes effort, but you can do it. Learning effective communication skills now will also help you in the other relationships you have throughout your life, whether with a boss, teacher, relative, friend, coworker, or someone you're dating.

Getting along with your family, particularly your parents, can ease the stress of being a teenager; not getting along will only add more. Do what you can on your end to get along. Just try it. The results might surprise your parents and even yourself.

Getting Through Difficult Situations

You already know that life can be tough when you're a teenager. There are many new things to think about and more and more decisions to make. You're not an adult yet, but you're not a kid either. Sometimes you are at a point where you want to grow up and your parents won't let you. Other times, your parents want you to grow up and take more responsibility, and you're just not quite ready. It *can* be tough.

Peer pressure, school, friends and enemies, members of the opposite sex, sports and activities: all of these things bring separate challenges, and many times, it's hard to take. The stress of being an adolescent takes its toll on many teenagers, and many of them withdraw socially, turn to drugs or alcohol, rebel by acting out, or take their own lives. None of these things are the answer.

According to the Centers for Disease Control, suicide is the second leading cause of death among people between the ages of fifteen and twenty-four, with approximately six thousand successful attempts each year. In the U.S. alone, among all age groups, a suicide occurs once every eleven minutes. Worldwide, that figure is one suicide every forty seconds (source: World Health Organization). Suicide is not the answer.

It shouldn't even be an option. You're on this earth for a reason, and you'll leave it when it's your time—not before.

The most important thing to remember, no matter what you are going through, is this phrase: This, too, shall pass. In order to get through to better, more positive things in your life, sometimes it's necessary to go through pain. But it *will* get better. I guarantee it. Nothing that comes your way is so difficult that you cannot handle it. You have to keep in mind that all things that happen to you in life bring a lesson with them. All things teach an important lesson if you just step back and look at what the situation is showing you. You'll get through whatever it is, and it will make you stronger and wiser. You'll look back and be proud of yourself for making it, and sometimes you'll even be able to laugh at the past.

Remember, too, that you aren't alone. There are guardian angels all around you. Your higher spirit is with you at all times. All you have to do is ask for assistance, and you *will* receive it. Trust, believe, and never give up.

Respecting People's Property

Respecting people's property is a life lesson that you should already know by now. This basic principle was most likely (hopefully) taught to you at a young age by your parents and other people you spent time with. They taught you to take good care of things you borrow and not to vandalize or steal. These are things that should be so ingrained in your head that you don't have to think twice about.

But, unfortunately, some people your age haven't been taught these important things, or they choose to ignore them. They go through life trampling through other people's flower gardens, so to speak. They may even try to convince you to join in.

Perhaps they shoplift. "Come on," they say. "It's fun. It's easy. No one will ever know. You'll get this cool thing without having to pay for it. Shoplifting is cool. It doesn't hurt anybody or anything." But you don't do it. In fact, you don't even have to think twice about it because you've been taught well. You have morals and principles that you believe in, and you know that stealing is wrong in any way, shape, or form.

But what do you do? How do you convince your friend not to do it? Try this approach. Say: "It may be fun to *you*, but to *me*, it's wrong. It's not worth the risk to me. I don't want to be a part of it, because I'll get in trouble, too." Don't bag on your friend or be critical. Just state your beliefs and stand up for them. I wouldn't be surprised if your friend has a sudden change of heart and decides not to do it.

Of course, there's always that chance that they'll tease you or call you a chicken. Do not—and I repeat, *do not*—let it bother you. And if they still decide to lift something, get away from them. You can get in trouble just by being with them. So get away. It may even be a good time to reevaluate the people you're hanging out with. Do you really want to be around people like that? It's just something to think about.

Time for another little story. This one is about my dad, and took place when I was in the second or third grade. At that time, I was in Girl Scouts, and our troop met after school each Thursday at the scout house in Kelley Park. After the meetings, I walked about four blocks to my dad's office and he would give me a ride home. One day on the way to the office, I passed by some pretty flowers in a woman's yard. I stopped and picked a few, never thinking for a minute that I was doing anything wrong. When I got to the office, Dad asked where I'd gotten the flowers.

"In that lady's yard on the corner," I said, proudly clutching my little bouquet.

"Did she say you could pick them?" he said as we got into his car.

"Well, no. She wasn't outside," I responded.

"That's stealing," Dad said.

"No, it's not," I argued. "It's just some flowers."

He seemed to be getting more upset as I continued arguing with him, insisting that it was no big deal. I noticed that he was driving toward the police station. "Where are we going?" I asked.

"I'm going to take you in to talk to the police. They can tell you whether it's stealing."

"No! Dad. Come on. I didn't know I was doing anything wrong. I'm sorry." I was thinking, *Man, this is crazy. It's no big deal. He is really overreacting,* but I was scared at the same time, and I realized that what he was saying was true. The flowers I had picked belonged to someone. They were a part of a garden that had taken lots of time and effort, and the results of that work were something that the woman probably looked at and enjoyed with pride each and every day. I had taken part of that away, without asking.

"Dad, I'm sorry," I said, pleading with him one more time not to take me into the station.

"Are you?" he asked.

"Yes," I said.

"Do you promise not to steal anything ever again?"

"Yes, I promise," I said, and I meant it.

Now, when I look back on that, I see what a valuable lesson I learned that day. Maybe Dad did go a little bit overboard. It may have been scare tactics, but you know what? It worked. I have never stolen anything in my entire life (except those flowers), and I never will. Never.

The same thing applies not only to stealing, but also to anything that belongs to someone else. Take care of it. If you borrow or use something, give it back in better shape than when you got it if there's any way you can. Learn the lesson of respecting other people's property, and live it, every single day.

Preserving Your History

Preserving your history is probably not something you think about too much right now. You've got your whole life ahead of you. Why do you need to start keeping track of it now? That's a good question. But I have a good answer for you, and that answer is because you'll be glad you did. I know. I know. By now, you're getting tired of hearing me tell you to do things now because you'll be glad later. But listen to me. I'm not telling you these things just to hear my head rattle. It's never too early (or too late) to do things to benefit yourself. You are the most important person in your life.

Here are a few relatively simple ways that you can start preserving your history—today.

1. Keep a journal. Keeping a journal is a great idea and a very simple thing to do. Probably the hardest part is just getting started and then making it a _____ (you know the word). It can be one of the best ways to sort through problems and come to decisions about all kinds of things going on in your life. Putting your feelings and ideas on paper allows you to see things more clearly, in many cases, and helps you to look back days, weeks, months, or even years later

and note the progress you've made. A journal is an excellent counselor for a teenager and is something that I recommend you do throughout your entire life.

What do you write about? Anything and everything—whatever you want. Write about what you did that day, who you spent time with, secrets you don't want anyone else to know, inner struggles, and personal triumphs. It's important to put the date on each entry, so that when you look back later, you'll know when you wrote it. Just remember that there are no right or wrong things to write about. It's your journal, and you can fill it with anything you want.

Because I think keeping a journal is such a good idea, I'm even going to help you get started. At the back of this book are some blank pages for you to use as your own personal journal (you can thank me later). When those pages are full, pick out a journal in a style you like and start a brand-new one. Write away and enjoy writing about yourself.

2. Make a scrapbook. Scrapbooking can be a fun, worthwhile thing to do, and can be done as a hands-on book or on many online sites. What better way to preserve your personal memories of special (and ordinary) moments with friends and family? It's fairly inexpensive, and can be done on an ongoing basis. When done hands-on,

you can fill your scrapbook with all kinds of things: letters, cards, ticket stubs, brochures, drawings, and photos, of course. You'll want to write details beside each item, including the date and the people involved. Years later, when you look back, you'll be transported back in time to when the event happened, and you'll get to relive it over and over, vividly, in your memories.

Organize your photos. If you just can't get into making a scrapbook, at least get your pictures organized. I encourage you to print your favorite pictures, so you have a hard copy. So many people never save or print the pictures on their phones and devices, and they can be lost forever if it's not done. If you do print your pictures, try to get them into a book or album and write down the names and details. It's amazing how quickly details can be forgotten if they aren't written down. Not only will you get to enjoy the pictures more if they're in an album, your children and their children and on and on will also get a better idea of what kind of person you really were.

By preserving your history with permanent keepsakes, such as journals, scrapbooks, and photo albums, you are able to celebrate your memories over and over again as often as you choose. You are also allowing others, years from now, to celebrate you and your life.

Bridging the Generation Gap

Have you ever heard of the generation gap? What exactly is it? The generation gap is the difference in attitudes and ideas between generations of people, such as children, their parents, and their grandparents. Most likely, you've already experienced this, even if you didn't know that there was a name for it. The generation gap has been around in one way or another since the beginning of time, and it will most likely continue forever, as people's lives change from year to year with the development of new inventions, ideas, and ways of thinking.

So how do you build a bridge that can connect you to your parents or grandparents when you both think so differently? For starters, one of the things we have already talked about comes into play: communication. Communication can be a very effective bridge builder. Just talking about your differences can help. Not only will you both gain insight, but also you might even get a new perspective on whatever the situation is.

Another good bridge builder is interaction. Interact with people from different generations, including both older *and* younger people. You can really learn a lot from older people (remember my friend Irel from the section on smoking?). You'll see how different life is today than it was ten, twenty, thirty, or fifty years ago. You'll also be surprised to discover the many similarities between the two. Older people want nothing more than to share and pass on what they have learned. Spend as much time as you can with your grandparents (or an older person you think is interesting). Sit down with them and visit. Ask questions. Look through old photographs. Visit someplace with them that holds special memories. Listen to what they say and accept it with open arms. Both of you will benefit.

Spending time with people younger than you can also be a great experience. Younger people want nothing more than to learn from you. Little children (including little brothers and sisters) watch your every move. They want to be like you. Show them how to do something they've never learned from anyone else. Take them someplace fun. Play hard. Teach by example how to live life to the fullest. You can make a difference in the lives of the younger generation, as you help guide them on their way down life's path.

You'll probably find that learning to "bridge the gap" can be an enjoyable experience, and one that doesn't have to be difficult. It will also help you later on when you have children, grandchildren, or even great-grandchildren of your own.

Hey, Jennye!

We've come to the end of our journey. I hope you've enjoyed the trip, learning and laughing a little along the way. It's my hope that the words on these pages will help you, at least in some small way, to get through your teenage years a bit easier. I know it can be difficult because "I've been there, done that."

After you've read this book and completed your personal journal in the back, save it. Put it in a safe place and look at it every now and then for reminders and helpful tips on living your life to the fullest. Look back at your journal once in a while and remember what you were going through as you wrote down your thoughts, fears, hopes, and dreams.

Reflect on those times and look for the lessons that came from each thing—both good and bad—that you went through.

And someday, maybe you'll feel like sharing this book with your own little sister or even your own daughter. By then, you'll have had many, many interesting experiences. You'll be wiser, braver, stronger, and smarter with each new challenge that you have faced and overcome along your way.

Unfortunately, you can read all the books in the world, and study until your brain explodes, and you'll never become an expert on life and its ups and downs. There are no experts. But by enjoying life, savoring each moment, and following the inner guidance that your heart gives you, you'll become just as close to being an expert as anyone else ever has. Take care, Jennye. I wish you all the best life has to offer.

About The Author

Michelle Moses has been interested in children and their well-being since long before she had children of her own. Her writing is clever, and to-the-point and never ceases to be amusing and informative. Michelle's writing includes both fiction and nonfiction, short stories, poetry, and cookbooks.

Notes to Self